Millionaire for Teens

Stay Blessed.
Lots of Love - Abdullah.

Millionaire

For

Teens

Abdullah Ahmad

Connect With Abdullah:

Instagram: @dtmdmagician

Email: dtmdmagician@gmail.com

**ISBN-13:
978-1548370824**

**ISBN-10:
1548370827**

The vision's getting clearer, no more teenage fever.
- Abdullah Ahmad

This book is dedicated to all the true doggos, love you.

12 THINGS THIS BOOK CAN HELP YOU ACHIEVE

A more productive and positive outlook on life.

○

The ability to live your life full of energy.

○

Self-love, self-belief and self-confidence.

○

The ability to meditate and visualise effectively.

○

A better quality of sleep.

○

A more present life of fewer worries and more creations.

○

A happier life.

○

The quality of fearlessness.

○

Your first lucid dream.

○

The correct mind set for the acquisition of wealth.

○

The ability to educate yourself.

○

A sense of inner peace.

CONTENTS

HOW
THIS
BOOK
WAS
WRITTEN
AND
WHY

'Millionaire for Teens' is truly a manifestation from my subconscious mind. I have always dreamed of my end goal. Me as an old man, looking back over my life's achievements. In the course of my life I will have, a clothing brand, many properties all over the world, a few other businesses creating passive income for me, unconditional freedom in all areas, a warm and loving family with children and grandchildren, many dear friendships, sublime health, inner peace, alchemistic abilities, huge social media accounts, the ability to manifest anything I desire when I desire, a sense of satisfaction and fulfilment, a house by the beach with a private skate park and a few books written and published.

Writing a book has always been one of my life goals. I've always wanted to do it but I never truly believed in my ability to write a book especially when I saw my school grades for the 'English' subject. My mind used to ask questions like these: Who would even read it? Why would anyone listen to what I had to say? What would I write about? When would I ever have the time to write a book? Where would I print it and how would I ever get it published? So for a long time I saw writing a book as an unreachable goal. I didn't think of it as truly being possible for me. My mind was telling me this and that definitely assisted in my putting off the goal.

Then one day, everything changed. I came to a realisation after finding a fourteen year old author and entrepreneur named, Caleb Maddix. He earned over $100,000 while being fourteen years old. He spoke on his YouTube channel of how he had always wanted to write a book and one day he just did – he talks in depth about it in his video. That book truly changed his life and the lives of each reader. Since then he's written numerous other books. He also inspired me to write my own book. Why would I wait? I have value to give so I may as well give it. I have always loved creating anyways so this would simply be another project for me. I made the decision to finish it by summer, approximately 8 months later.

Bear in mind, I have never written a book before. I had no clue how to format a book, edit a book, design a book cover, write poetically or keep the reader's attention. I didn't need to know either. All I needed to write this book was my end goal – completing this book and self-publishing it -, my plan of action – daily and weekly goals -, belief that it will all happen and work out, my ability to visualise the end product before it even existed and my desire to learn, grow and spread true value.

I worked every single day in silence for months with my end goal in mind. I just wanted to help as many teenagers as possible to see the opportunities that they pass by every second. I want to play my part in ending the complaining habit and swapping it with creating. I wanted - and still want to this day - teenagers to realise their full potential and learn how to materialise that to become their greatest self.

I will not be alive on this earth for all of eternity although I am confident that my creations will. My goal is not to live forever; it is to create mounds of value that will. I would rather impact one million people positively than earn one million euro. All I truly want is unconditional freedom. Enjoy reading this book as much as I did writing it. - Abdullah "i'm just doing me, man."

Chapter 1

DOING ME

All we have in this life is merely our mind and this very moment. Ironically, our mind has the power to change this very moment and this very moment has the power to change our mind. However, we have the power to choose which changes which. Above all we need not worry about anything as we are in control of our future.

STRENGTHS AND WEAKNESSES

The only person we can truly compete with is our past selves. We are our only competition. Therefore, we must at least know and be honest with ourselves. That's where **self–awareness** comes in to play. My personal definition of the phrase 'self–awareness' is, being bluntly honest with one's self in knowing personal strengths and weaknesses and acting upon them. Remember; never simply take notes – TAKE ACTION!

This definition can be interpreted as 'spend our time wisely by outbalancing it in favour of our strengths.' Time is our greatest asset and it must be treated with respect. We will dive deeper into the topic of time management throughout the course of this publication.

However, as of right now, YOU need to be fully honest with yourself. If for whatever reason, your ego is too great to allow you to be honest with yourself; you may as well lay this book down as you are reading this very sentence.

For those of us, who are capable of being honest with ourselves, let's proceed by grabbing some paper. Any blank sheet of paper will suffice. Now, draw a line straight down the middle of it. Title the left column **'Weaknesses'** and the right column **'Strengths'**. Write down at least 15 weaknesses and 15 strengths into the appropriate columns. Spend 10 minutes on each column and stay real. There's no point in us attempting to flatter ourselves. Sharing the data collected on this piece of paper with others is not recommended. With that being said, we'll only be fooling ourselves by not taking this first analysis seriously.

I'll include a few of my entries below for inspiration. After each strength and weakness I have given a detailed explanation of it for easy understanding. This is not necessary for you to imitate. The examples below are merely my own personal examples, not guidelines.

Strengths – I'm good at...

Public Speaking ~ I love talking to crowds. I find myself naturally gifted in the art of inspiring and motivating groups of people. Communicating ideas is one of my strengths.

Saving ~ I'm great at saving money *when I know where it's going and why*. I have developed very strong self-discipline. I do not let anything go under the radar, no matter how small. Saving is one of my strengths.

Designing Clothes ~ After two years of designing clothes on a daily basis, I grew significantly as a fashion designer. I now find a profound beauty in giving each and every detail a purpose. The clothes that I've designed incorporate the countless expressions of myself. What I release this year was most likely designed upwards of 18 months prior to its release. The best is yet to come!

Brainstorming ~ I am like a machine when it comes to generating ideas, once I'm in a brainstorming environment. I can come up with solutions to any problem *when asked the right questions by the right people.* This of course is a highly applicable craft.

Focus ~ I can sit down for 10 minutes, plan the next three hours and then stick directly to them plans until the time is over – without being distracted at all. I feel that focus is similar to a muscle my body – the more I train it, the stronger it gets. As they say, 'practice makes perfect.' I have most definitely been putting in the practice.

Selling ~ As an entrepreneur, it's extremely important that I can sell efficiently. Before I ever started any businesses of my own, I've always recognised the recurring ability to sell – goods and/or services – effectively within myself. Whether it was selling me and my time as a magician to an audience, selling baguettes to parents at a school bake sale or selling custom sweatshirts to celebrities, the core principles of selling have always been the same for me. Selling is certainly one of my strong points.

Singing ~ Musically, I know what sounds good to my ears, just as I know what looks good, to my eyes – fashion wise. Music, among all other forms of art, is appreciated and respected highly in my life and is a big part of my lifestyle. I have an ear for aesthetically pleasing sounds – to me. I love singing.

Social Media ~ Without a doubt, I wouldn't be half as successful as I am today without my social media skills. I have invested hundreds of hours in the expansion of my knowledge on social media marketing and generating traffic. It has payed off abundantly.

Making Definite Decisions ~ I make definite decisions and stick to them. No matter what, once I've made my mind up, it's staying that way. This helps me value my successes and analyse my failures more carefully. When we make quick, definite, decisions and stick to them, it truly boosts our self-confidence and self-belief. It shows ourselves that we are serious about the decision.

For example, how many people do you know that 'tried' to quit eating unhealthily? When attempting to quit unhealthy eating, unless you make a definite decision that you will never eat unhealthily again, you will end up relapsing after some time. You cannot try to make a decision; you must desire the outcome of your decision and have full faith in your ability to endure it. Otherwise, you may as well not bother 'trying' as it most definitely will not work for long. We must make these decisions for ourselves and to better ourselves. Definite decisions are highly beneficial in relation to business.

Networking ~ I'm known for creating strong relationships with people. You either really like me or really don't. I create new, strong relationships everywhere I go. As they say, your vibe attracts your tribe! *Your network predicts your net worth.*

Weaknesses – I'm bad at…:

Taking Orders ~ I hate to take orders from other people. This is probably why I feel so uncomfortable in school. In school, I am told how to think, what to think and when to think. I must answer to 'teachers'. I must do what these 'teachers' tell me to do. I must believe what these 'teachers' tell me to be true. 'Teachers' with different beliefs and morals to me. Some of these 'teachers' hate their lives and still have the audacity to try and tell me how to live my life and what I am and/or am not capable of doing. Also, the actual material which we are taught in school is, for the most part, irrelevant to anything that I aspire to achieve. I wouldn't be surprised if you weren't happy with the 'educational system' either.

We should've at least heard of the *'seven hermetic principles'* by the time we've finished secondary school (high school). Why are the names of war leaders chanted and not the names of creators, good doers, philanthropists, writers and speakers such as the great Napoleon Hill, the one and only Jim Rohn, the spectacular Dale Carnegie, Earl

Nightingale, Les Brown, Zig Ziglar, Andrew Carnegie, Henry Ford, John D. Rockefeller, Steve Jobs, Mark Zuckerberg, Bill Gates, Benjamin Franklin, Charles M. Schwab etc.? Personally, I do not see any relevance in the current formal system of 'education' – in Ireland. I don't agree with it for what *I allowed* it do to me. I've since fully recovered although many teenagers do not recover, ever. It is a fact that when we are **forced** to think other people's thoughts, we begin to resist them as NOTHING FORCED EVER WORKS. Keep in mind that *resistance will only make stronger.* This resistance leads us into overthinking. For me, my overthinking had manifested in the form of depression and sometimes even suicidal thoughts. At one point of my life between November 2016 and January 2017, I was dangerously emotional during school hours. While in school I would truly want to die. I didn't want to live through the rest of my school years anymore as I knew that I did not belong there. I found myself stuck within a combination of bullying, misunderstanding, very low frequencies (low energy – partly from massive sleep deprivation, lack of motivation and of course the outer energies from my peers which I was soaking up), isolation and no sense of belonging. For upwards of eight hours every school day, I would feel and think in this destructive manner. However the moment that I entered my home, my subconscious mind's focus would kick back in – as I programmed it to – and remind me of my goals and my life purpose. Thankfully at that time I had somewhat realised a purpose for my life – it has since changed.

Afterschool, I was a totally different person. I sincerely loved and truly appreciated my life. I was grateful for every opportunity coming my way. I was embodying my true, unfiltered, uncensored self. I was productive. I stayed up late educating myself. I spent hours proactively creating and learning about what really mattered to me. I truly worked behind the scenes. *I educated myself.* I would spend hours listening to personal development lectures from the best of the best – in my opinion – Earl Nightingale, Jim Rohn, Zig Ziglar, Bob Proctor etc. and read REAL books like, 'Think and Grow Rich', by Napoleon Hill, 'How to Win Friends and Influence People', by Dale Carnegie and 'The Power of Now', by Eckhart Tolle. The lectures and books gave me a sense of belonging. They gave me a sense of control and purpose. They taught me that my life was in my own hands and I am not obliged to do anything. It rooted the fact that; I wouldn't have to go through school and then college and then work for money in a job where I either wouldn't like or where it wouldn't allow me the freedom that I would want deep within the root of my subconscious and my conscious minds. A recent survey showed that around 80% of Americans are working at jobs that they are not happy in. I began to realise that the widely accepted and preached 'safe and secure way of living' was not at all my only option. It was and is not the only way to live. On the other hand, I can choose to manifest my desires. The choice is all in my possession. *I can either put in the work or settle.* Work for your desired life or settle for a mediocre one. One that you know is not reaching your full potential. By work I do not mean work a day job! 100% of the people who openly disagree with that statement have settled. Settling is not a bad thing unless you are unsatisfied with your life. If all you want is a small house on a farm in the countryside and that's what you settle for, then in my eyes, you are living a very successful life. You are living out your desires – 95% of people never achieve that. Happiness should be our number one priority. Note that true, lasting happiness comes only from within, NOT FROM MATERIAL THINGS, therefore, settling for a lifestyle below what you are capable of acquiring shouldn't hinder your happiness if your happiness is from the true source. The problem is, most people haven't even found themselves yet, don't mind their inner happiness!

Long story short, I hate to take orders as it does not feel right. *I work best **with** people, not **for** them.*

Wasting Time ~ As much as I preach about not wasting time and how you must spend your time wisely, I myself waste time every single day. There are almost always at least two hours every day that are wasted (excluding the time spent sleeping). I am working on reducing this time and am seeing daily positive results.

Arguing ~ When someone gets me worked up – which thankfully is a rare occurrence – I will argue until I 'win', even though my studies have shown me that arguments are never truly won, this can waste unreasonable volumes of time. I'm trying to replace my impulsive responses with more relaxed, accepting responses as deep down, whether the speaker is correct or not, I really do not care. My ego may see it as an opportunity to declare a public display of dominance although, my love fuelled body does not care.

Exercise ~ I need to work on my fitness and overall physical health. I skate every day. I love my penny board! I find skating thoroughly enjoyable although I know that it's not enough to maintain a fit body. When I turn sixteen, I will start attending the gym daily.

Eating Healthily ~ My diet is truly in need of some major reviewing. I consume far too little fruits and vegetables at the moment. By the time this book is in your hands, this issue will be cleared up. I have a diet plan for the summer of 2017 and have made the definite decision to stick to it. In the future I will experiment with a vegan diet and lifestyle although I will take my nourishment journey in baby steps.

Sleeping ~ I rarely ever get more than five or six hours of sleep per night. I feel within myself that I am in need of more sleep. I am constantly working and reworking my schedules to combat this although I currently value the completion of my planned projects and my long term success higher than my need for sleep. As I type this sentence, it is 00:39am and today's schedule told me to turn off all electronics and sleep at 11pm. I don't ever stop, even for sleep, once I get going.

Controlling My Ego ~ This is an ongoing journey for me. I am always working to eliminate and control my ego. There needs to be the correct balance between subconsciously knowing what your worth and consciously thinking about what you're worth. Mark Zuckerberg is truly inspirational in my eyes as he never totally allowed his ego to take control of him, even in his early years, showing once again that age is not the variable, usually maturity is. Acquiring a massive fortune by the age of 19 would get to most people's head although Mark dealt with it very well. Most local peoples that I have worked with have had what I perceived as bigger egos than Kanye West with

0% of his achievements. Some of the 'ego driven aliens' that I have worked with, especially in the 'fashion industry', have been so egotistical and haven't had anything to back up their huge egos. They are literally nobodies. Having 400 likes on Instagram does not make you famous or give you a reason to treat people with little to no respect. Having 1,000,000 likes on Instagram does not make you famous or give you a reason to treat people with little to no respect. Likes simply don't matter. Either work and create your own level – like Kanye and Mark – or settle and know your place. I personally don't think of any celebrities when I think of Ireland other than maybe Connor McGregor – and he isn't even accepted or appreciated by a substantial fraction of the Irish population. I don't think he gets enough praise for the way he has represented Ireland – so why do so many lazy underachievers think that they are above everyone else when we are all equal? I believe that all humans are equal no matter how successful or lazy.

*If everyone's life is **unfair**, doesn't that make everyone's life **fair?*** We are all one; ego does not need to live within us. We just need a humble confidence.

Judging People ~ I judge everyone silently. I will openly admit that. I know that I am not the only one either. I am working to accept more than I judge. This will save me masses of time in the long run. I categorise everyone as a 95%, a 5% or a 1%.

When someone is a 95%, they are not special or valuable to me in any way as they have no substance. Everywhere I go, I will meet 95%ers in different bodies. They are all the same. They're found everywhere. They have no judgment for themselves and everything that they do is simply an imitation. The clothes they wear, the way they walk, the way they talk, the type of language they use, the music they listen to, their opinions on basically everything and anything, the books they read, the places they go, their ideas of fun, the way they spend their money, the way they get their money, their levels of happiness and energy... I could literally go on all day. 99.999999999999999999% of humans are brought up to become a 95%er. That's probably why they make up for 95% of the population; the corporate robots.

Then we have the 5%ers. 5% of people know their worth. They know their potential and they know that they have infinite possibilities for their lives. These people are not all the same. They come in many different forms. They know what they are capable of and they know that it is possible for them. However they never act on what they learn. They just know what they can do but *they never do anything*. The thought of them achieving is enough for them to become filled with ego. They allow themselves to become complacent because they know that they can do it. They never actually do anything though. They're the type of person who will tell you that they are working instead of actually working. *They would rather look good than do good.* These people have a lot of potential to join the 1%, with the correct mentorship. I spent a lot of time in this category.

Finally, the '1% group'. It is most certainly not 1% of the population. It's at most, 0.00001%. I meet around one new person from this group every few months and I proactively look for them online. In person, I've physically met four of these people. These are the people who do more than they say. People may or may not know that they are working on something. They work in silence and usually alone too. They are highly educated in their fields. They know their potential and work towards achieving it every single day. They are not easy to come across. They lose interest in relationships with people who are not in the same category as themselves quite easily. They work well with likeminded people. They value their time and their long term happiness highly. They are the most productive group of people. They are doers and achievers. They are active and energetic. They have freedom.

Formal education teaches you to be a 95 percenter.

Self-education teaches you to be a 1 percenter.

ANALYSIS

Now, analyse your lists. What do you notice about them? Which column was easier to write? Which column took longer for you to write? Right now, think of one method to overcome each of your first five entries on the 'Weaknesses' column. How can you get better?

How do you feel about yourself now that you've constructively analysed where you truly are? Many people are surprised by the amount of strengths that they find when they make an effort to recall them. Read through your strengths again and truly be grateful for each and every one of them. Realise how much potential you truly have. Realise that self-love is needed in order to fulfil your true potential. After completing this analysis, you will come to the conclusion that you cannot honestly say, 'There's nothing to love about me.' Love yourself. Say, 'I love everything about my ever improving self!' With conviction at least five times every day. If you do not love yourself, you will attract the wrong people circumstances and things into your life – we will plunge deeper into this topic within the following chapters. Love always.

LOVE MANY, TRUST FEW AND ALWAYS PADDLE YOUR OWN CANOE.

My grandmother would repeatedly recite this phrase for me anytime I told her of business or personal relationship mishaps. It has been proven highly effective time and time again in my relationships. I've only recently broken down its root meaning.

Love Many.

Love is important. Love has the highest frequency of all energies. When you truly feel the emotion of love, your energy is at a peak. In this universe, everything at its most basic form is energy. The energies that we emit will be attracted to us like a magnet. 'Like attracts like.' Not only do you get what you give but you get it multiplied. *Giving starts the receiving process*. While emitting the energy of love, we are attracting love and much more loving, high energy feelings and other physical objects into our life that are in line with the energy of love – as that is what we are emitting. This is the Law of Attraction.

Trust Few.

Trust must be earned, it cannot be bought. People commonly mistake trust for the duration of the relationship – 'I trust Jake as I've known him for years.' Maybe 'Jake' has been plotting on how to exploit you for them years. Trust is not a test of time. Time does not exist. All we have is now. Therefore, if 'Jake' has been trustworthy for three years or your whole life up until today, that doesn't mean he won't change tomorrow – without you knowing. Pay close attention to the people you ensure your trust in. Who do you trust? 'Who do I trust?' Ask yourself this. Whether it's a business or a personal relationship, what have they done to receive your trust? Why them of all people? Do they deserve your trust? Would you trust them with your money, your clothes, your ideas, your secrets, your bank details, your company's shares, your reputation, your feelings, your most vulnerable self, your social media details, your emotions, your good and bad habits, your time, your love, your thoughts, your mind set, your talents, your name, your stories etc. If we only trusted those who we could trust fully, every relationship – business or personal – would flourish beautifully and emit honest, loving energy. Emotionally open and trusting relationships are always the healthiest. Keep your distance from those people who you can't fully express yourself around – this may be most or all of your 'friends.' You will feel when a relationship is meant to be. Trust your feelings. Trust yourself. Trust few.

Always Paddle Your Own Canoe.

The ideology of this phrase sparked the thought of Joker Clothing's 'DoingMe' collection. Do you. In my eyes the phrase, 'Always paddle your own canoe', emphasises the need to live for you. Not your friends, not your family, not your business, not your dog, you. This is your life, nobody else's. We must promise ourselves to live for ourselves. This does not mean that we disregard everyone or be selfish or self-centred. This means, we must do what we feel. If we feel like our message needs to be heard, we will make it heard. We will not be discouraged by the negativity of our relatives and peers. It is 2017 now. Literally everything is possible. That's simply a fact. It's possible. Our dreams are possible to achieve. If anybody tells you otherwise, frankly, they are wrong. There's no doubt in my mind that you can achieve all of your goals – when you work both hard and smart for them. However make sure that they are *your* goals. Refrain from letting your surroundings influence your dreams. There are zero limits. You are worthy and capable of achieving all of your goals no matter how big they are.

TRUST YOURSELF 100%

We live a balanced, consistent & purposeful lifestyle once we know and trust ourselves with every atom in our bodies. The outcomes are astonishing when we come to trust ourselves. We eliminate procrastination, doubt & fear from our lives. We see the opportunities that are all around us. Failure no longer exists, only learning opportunities. We open our eyes to the beauty that lies within our immediate environment. We begin to truly love. We become alchemists. We realise that 'good' and 'bad' only exists if we believe in it. We see the possibility of inciting abundance. We open up to the possibility of inner peace. We become consumed by gratitude and love. Our energies are consistently at an all-time high. We feel alive. We live.

THIS IS YOUR LIFE

When we desire something, whether it be a certain 'dream car', the perfect soulmate, an amount of money etc. we must get serious with ourselves. You may have heard the saying, 'dreams don't work unless you do!' this is most certainly a fact. You can dream and visualise and affirm to yourself all that you want but you must take action to start seeing changes.

While on the journey of taking action towards our personal dreams, we will begin to realise some or all of the following; we are surrounded by so many distractions, the system in which we are a part of does not want us to succeed, we will have to work in silence or we will be ridiculed and discriminated against, when people don't see themselves being able to accomplish something, they won't see it for you either, the more time we spend working by ourselves, the more we enjoy our own company and the greater level of inner peace and acceptance we acquire, confidence in ourselves and our work is necessary for the acquisition of our goals, formal education will not teach us what we need to know to acquire what we desire, time is the most valuable commodity on this planet, WE CAN DO MORE, we are not fulfilling our full potential yet, we are capable of packing our time with more value, we are working harder than most although we are not outworking ourselves, practice definitely polishes our skills, we have infinite potential, our goals and desires are very possible to achieve, in order to work as well as we are capable, we MUST get the correct nutrition and exercise, our inputs lead to our outputs, money does not bring happiness, happiness brings money, all forms of communication are valuable, we must perfect our communicational skills by practicing them vigorously and when we act as though we have already achieved our goals, we become serious in ourselves and want to work for them even more.

I have come to realise these and many other truths. The journey of fulfilling our desires is a truly exciting journey to undergo. Much more exciting and rewarding than the regular 'go to school, get a job, have a family, have grandkids, retire and die' lifestyle. When we chase our dreams, we wake up every morning with enthusiasm and an abundance of energy. We are driven and focused. We leave distractions behind us and move forward in OUR lives.

While perusing our dreams, we may come to difficult decisions. Friends are asking us to come out to a party but we have yet to complete your goal for today. We know we have to work on our dreams but we also want to see our friends and have fun. We don't want to say no although we are serious about our goals. This is when our self-discipline will be tried and tested. This is when we need to get serious with ourselves and ask us what is really more important. Do we really value temporary happiness over long term prosperity? If so then we may as well give up on our goals and desires now. We will have the choice to sacrifice for our future. It is a choice. The more sacrifices we make, the easier it gets and the more serious we become on the fulfilment of our desires. When we are truly serious and have full faith in our ability to realise our desires, we will make sacrifices with ease. It can be hard at the start however we must think about our priorities. This does not mean that we should cut everyone out of our life; it means we should have a small circle of likeminded friends who we can grow with rather than a group of 'friends' who will criticise and ridicule us and will get in the way of our dreams. Following your dreams can be lonely. You will learn to love your own company.

DOING ME

The phrase 'DoingMe' implies putting yourself and your goals before anyone or anything else in the most unselfish of ways. As I practiced what I preached in full, I found myself awfully lonely for a time. This was the result of being selfish with my time. Yes, before – when I only took my time for myself – I was much more productive and driven although I was truly lonely beneath it all. This was mentally unhealthy. A couple months later I went through a deep stage of depression as a result. After this experience I realised that it is important to share your time with others but only with people who are special to you. Choose these people carefully. People who share positive energy with you are the best candidates in helping you both grow and prosper. Be yourself around everyone. This way you will find people on the same level and energetic frequency as you. Stop altering yourself for other people; *do not shrink yourself for those who refuse to grow.*

Do you.

"okay but presence solves the problem"

Chapter 2

Now

'Inspired By the Boy Who Allowed'
The Power of Presence & Effective Meditation

Inside this chapter is the secret to staying present and living in the now! You are about to learn how to eliminate the majority of your worries and fears. This may sound exciting although I must admit; every script that I have ever read on this topic has either lost my attention or lost my interest after some time. These writings can be very hard to understand – and write – at times as they must be worded very precisely. Eckhart Tolle even says something along the lines of, 'if you do not understand the meaning of the words used, at least feel them.' I don't even fully understand what he means even by that although when I read his books or listen to his lectures, I can most certainly feel his teachings on a deeper level, almost as though my inner body understands the truth of his words although my conscious mind cannot define it. He uses the word 'being' quite frequently. One day while reading his bestseller entitled, 'The Power of Now', I was quite amused when he said that the conscious mind will try to define 'being' and place it into a mental box for you to consciously understand although the trueness of being cannot be mentally or consciously understood, it can only be felt. You either are *being* in a certain moment or you are not.

With all of that in mind, persist through the boredom and restlessness of the following chapter. The teachings in it will greatly assist you on your journey towards success and fulfilling your desires. When you get bored, refocus. Even though I tried to make it as understandable as possible, when you cannot understand, read on and trust that you will come to understand. Enjoy!

Why We Should Live In the Now

Presence is the key. There is a power greater than ourselves emitted from those of us who live in the now. When we live in the now, we are present. We are living only in this exact moment. We are not thinking or worrying. We are just here and merely observing. Our worries disappear. The illusion of right and wrong – positive and negative – leaves our minds. Our eyes open to the beauty surrounding us. Every detail is seen, heard, smelled, tasted and felt.

Anxiety is unheard of. Thoughts slip away. Time passes. Movements slow. Colours blossom. Birds glide. Clouds float. Ideas visit, opportunities too. Inspiration lands before us. Life is lived. Stress dies peacefully. We are neither happy nor sad. We are simply enough. We are balanced. We are appreciated by our surroundings. We are infinite. We are at peace within ourselves. Everything is noticed. Everything is. We are.

The only things stopping us from living in the moment and recognising our inner peace and happiness are our thoughts. When we give our attention to what is actually happening rather than what our thoughts are telling us is happening, we become present. Imagine this scenario:

You're walking down the street and you hear a group of people shouting. Each of them is holding up a sign with their theory on it. They're all screaming the same thing:

"THE WORLD WILL END TOMORROW!"

You don't know what to think so you believe them. How would you feel? Afraid, sad, worried etc. you would definitely feel some form of emotions if you believed them. You just found out that today is the last day on earth! *The longer they shouted and chanted the more attention you gave to them and the more you allowed yourself to believe them. You keep on listening vigorously. You begin to feel very emotional.*

Now, imagine this scenario:

A man comes up to you on the street and he tells you that the world will end tomorrow. You think the man is crazy so you don't pay him much attention. How do you feel? You probably don't feel anything. *He keeps on talking and in an attempt to give you logical proof to back his statement. You stop giving him and his words any attention as you do not believe what he is saying. You don't think that his words are of any importance so you stop listening to him and continue with your day.*

What can we learn from those two stories?

When we believe the words of others to be true, we give them attention and allow those words to create emotions for us. On the flipside, when we do not believe the words of others to be true, we stop giving them attention and do not let them create emotions for us. It is the exact same for the words in our mind – our thoughts. When we believe our thoughts to be true, they take our attention and they create emotions for us, swiping us from the present moment. When we do not believe the thoughts and words in our mind to be true, we stop giving them focus and attention and they stop creating our emotions.

With that being said, when we desire to live in the moment, we must realise that believing our thoughts are true will take our attention. When we simply stop believing our thoughts, we will in turn stop giving them focus and stop allowing them to create emotions for us. This will allow you to focus all of your attention on the present moment.

Methods of Presence

There are many ways to become present. When we meditate properly, we are living in the now. Living in the now is in essence, being present. *When we are present, our thoughts are absent.* Our mind and body relaxes as one. Thankfully, meditation is not the only way to experience true presence!

The quickest way for me to become present and live in the now is to take deep, controlled breaths.

Step One ~ Inhale

Go ahead, yield a bottomless breath. How much air can your lungs clutch? Inhale with your nose. Presently acknowledge the stimulating feeling of life surging through your nostrils, down your trachea and flooding your lungs. Notice the areas of your body that inflate. Inspire until your lungs have reached their peak capacity.

Step Two ~ Exhale

Exhale via your mouth, not your lips but your whole mouth. Allow all of the tension and stress within the muscles of your body to leave alongside your breath. Allow your lungs to slowly deflate, feeling the build-up of emotions migrating from your body. Furthermore, notice the areas of your body falling as you deflate your lungs.

Step Three ~ Repeat

Once you've administered the full clearance of your lungs, give birth to a new breath. Renew step one by inhaling absolutely. Maintain a deep focus on your inner body and how it feels. Feel the energy within each and every muscle of your body. Sustain the spotlight on your body by mentally scanning – from your head to your toes – how each and every muscle and bone in your body feels. Fix your concentration on your skull, your eyes, your nose, your lips, your jaw, your neck and each vertebra in your spine etc. Inspect each expanse for any underlying tension. Examine the emotion in each individual muscle and bone of your body. Is it positive or negative? Is it stressed or at ease? Now, allow the reality to be. Allow your body to feel as it feels. Do not try and make any area feel better different. Just acknowledge it and allow it. Be grateful for the opportunity to realise how your body feels. Simply allow.

[DISCLAIMER] We mustn't try to count how many seconds our inhales and/or exhales are, as the aim of this exercise is to **allow** our thoughts to walk and run freely through our minds. We are not trying to resist nor hold onto any thoughts or feelings. We must remember that nothing is universally right or wrong. We must create our own moral guidelines for ourselves; therefore, the thoughts which we receive are only positive and/or negative if we have chosen for them to be. We are simply allowing our thoughts to flow like water down the stream of which we have labelled our imaginations.

Now that you've briefly experienced the feeling of presence, even just for a couple of seconds or milliseconds in between your breaths, you can work on creating a permanent stress free, present life. You must forget about the past and the future. Simply live now.

As I write this, I am sitting in a popular fast food chain in the heart of Dublin city. I'm taking a half hour break from being a 'hand model' for their milkshakes, breakfasts, burgers and chips. I am enjoying this moment. I can feel a slight waft of air blowing from the fans above me. I can hear the funky, chilled out music. I can feel the sole of my shoe digging into the back of my right thigh. I am present. There is nothing to worry about. My first Junior Cert examination is in less than 24 hours. Presently, there is nothing to worry about. Each second is a new one. Life goes on.

In forgetting about the past, we must realise that there is nothing that we can do to change it. Whatever has happened… happened. All we can do is merely analyse and reflect on the past. **We cannot change it**. Imagine this, *you're having an amazing day and then suddenly, you drop and smash your phone screen.*

Our immediate response is to curse and swear and become filled with anger and disappointment. How will that fix our screen? Forget about it. It's just a piece of glass. We can get a new one, maybe not the same day but we can replace it. At least we did not fall and smash a few bones!

Ten seconds have passed since you dropped your phone and you are still angry and aggressive.

Why? We must ask ourselves, 'why am I angry?' It's been ten whole seconds. We could have enjoyed a croissant in that time but instead we're spending the time being angry about something which we cannot and will not change in this moment. Move on. Time won't heal this one, so just forget about it. Play some great music and dance around the kitchen. We must do something to raise our energy levels. Remember: Doing nothing does nothing!

Now you're in a bad mood and everything that happens around you seems to magically piss you off. You're only looking at the negative sides of every situation. You're so distracted by the past that you accidentally walk into the door and stub your toe on it. You whole day is beginning to look like a waste all because of you choosing to dwell on the past. You start remembering all of the other bad things that made you curse and swear and act aggressively in the past. You are constantly reminded of how bad you feel and you relay your story to everyone you meet for the rest of the day. Your day is wasted.

It's a snowball effect. When we dwell on negativity, we begin to expect it. Therefore, we are only looking out for negativity. So when one bad thing happens, it will trigger another, just by thinking about it. We must do ourselves a favour and forget about it. Immerse yourself in nature. Start appreciating the beauty that surrounds you. *Nature has no admission fee.* It is necessary for us to do something that will break this cycle and make us happy again.

Know this: YOU DO NOT NEED A REASON TO BE HAPPY. With that being said, if you would like a reason to be happy, here's a few of my favourites:

You are alive.

You have eyes and/or ears to consume this book.

There is nature in your environment.

You have infinite potential.

You believe in yourself.

There is energy and blood flowing through your body.

Your heart is beating.

You have clothes to wear.

Birds sing for you for free!

You're capable of achieving anything you desire.

You're in control of your thoughts.

You control what you consume.

You are breathing in life!

All of the above are facts. Stop complaining and enjoy your life.

PRESENCE IS PRODUCTIVE

When we are living presently, we can become significantly more productive. We do not think about the future or the past. When we give ourselves tasks, they are completed with ease as nothing else enters our focus. All we have is now, so by staying present, we can get more done.

"i notice how you look at me"

Chapter 3

NOTICED
'Inspired By the Boy Who Realised'
The Power of Realisations, Work & Planning

This chapter expresses some of the many things that I have noticed. Reading and understanding this chapter will save you lots of time and many sufferings. It will help you to overcome a large volume of the road blocks that you will face throughout your journey towards your success. While reading 'NOTICED', acknowledge what is relatable to your life presently and become aware of what is not yet relatable. Do not become fearful, simply become aware.

HOW TO DEAL WITH REALISATIONS

While reading this book, you may begin to realise why certain things have happened in your life and why you are currently going through whatever it is that you are going through. This can be both exciting and scary. However you feel, just allow it and enjoy the mix of emotions. The first time I watched the movie 'The Secret' by Rhonda Byrne, I experienced dozens and dozens of realisations. It teaches that whatever situation we are in right now, we have attracted it to ourselves, no matter how good or bad it may seem. It taught me to take full responsibility of where my life is. 'The Secret' brought much awareness to the spiritual side of living, not just the physical side. After watching it, I was so excited and I felt like I was ready to take on the world – as I had the universe on my team.

I lost many friends as they did not realise what I had realised. I felt isolated as I was the only one who knew why things happened and how to take advantage of the universal laws. As I have said already, 'allow it to happen' When we are attracting the best version of ourselves, we may find ourselves gradually letting go of and/or drifting away from certain people, places, things and other attachments that we may have. *We must release the brake before we can move forward.* We must allow people to come and go in our life. When we make new realisations, we tend to make new friends and let go of old ones. Quite like when a phone with new features is released, we buy the new one and part with our old one. Sometimes we may wait until a few new generations are released before we let go of our old phone although we will have to let go of it at some stage as it no longer serves us. After letting go, our life will become easier and our productivity will rise.

We must allow our minds to ponder on our realisations until we have fully figured them out. We will notice many new things in our lifetime. We will notice how fake the majority of 'everything' is. *We only see what we are shown.* Therefore, we mustn't take anything as a fact. We must do our own research. Jim Rohn was too right when he said, "Be a student, not a follower." Ponder on our realisations.

WHAT I'VE NOTICED

I've had hundreds of realisations in the past four years. I appreciate them more now as they do not come as often. Every new realisation is more exciting than the last. I enjoy the mystery of wondering what something means or what the answer to something is. My life has always kept me asking questions, so far. I think we all love a good mystery. When information is simply handed to us, we can lose interest in it quite quickly. Although when we are required to search for the answers and put in an effort to acquire the information, we tend to appreciate it more and we are more enthusiastic about what we have found and worked for.

People Don't Care About You

I've noticed that a very microscopic number of people will ever truly have good intentions for you. Most people do not care about you or what you stand for. People are too caught up in their own business to have time to think/worry about yours. When people come to me asking, 'how can I stop caring what people think of me', I have to chuckle. They don't have time to think of you. They care and think about themselves, not you, so why would you spend your time thinking about them? There are probably only a handful of people who are thinking about you right now. Those are the people that should be on your mind! Also, keep in mind that when people make remarks about you, it is usually coming from an impulse not a thought or feeling. They say things to make themselves feel good, not to make you feel bad. They don't care about how you feel. When people criticise and ridicule you, simply allow it as arguments are never won by either party solely. You either have a win, win circumstance or one of your egos will be bruised, which will then reflect badly on the 'winner' of the argument – becoming a lose, lose circumstance. Just allow whatever is said – whether it is true or false – and move on with your life. If a reaction is what they're looking for, they will soon get bored. Life goes on, who cares what they say about you? *Be so busy being your true self that you have no more time to think or worry about what others might think.*

Don't Complain, Create

I've noticed how people are quick to complain about their circumstances and even quicker to refuse the idea of changing them. Any fool can complain and point out the wrong in a situation and most fools do. It takes honour and self-respect to analyse what is wrong and then make an effort to make it right. If it cannot be changed then learn to live with it. *Most people underestimate their abilities.* Accept it and move on, you'll save so much valuable time.

Money Plans Pay

I would highly recommend creating and following a money plan. Read and implement the remainder of this topic if you never want to be broke

– ever again. A money plan is basically a written document stating exactly how much money you have and how you are going to spend it. Do not mistake it for a budget, they are entirely different. Money plans are highly beneficial as you will always know how much money you have and where it is. I like to call my current money plan the 'sixty, thirty, ten plan'. It is implemented as follows:

60 – Sixty percent of all of my profits are put straight into savings. They are not touched until I need them for big investments. I always have a target of how much I want to save so that I am kept motivated to continue saving. My next big investment from my savings account will be the mass production of this very book. Saving is very important and is a phenomenal discipline to build up in your teenage years. The younger you are when you start saving, the more money you will accumulate!

30 – Thirty percent of all of my profits are put aside for investing. This could be in the form of buying and selling random stuff online, investing in advertising, investing in myself by buying a new personal development book, investing in my creativity by buying new arts and crafts tools, investing in marketing courses, investing in a skateboard to keep myself in shape and present, investing in a gym membership to keep myself fit, investing in a yoga mat in order to encourage myself to stay consistent in practicing yoga daily, investing in phone credit so that I have the freedom to call and text whenever I need to and I have internet everywhere I go, putting money aside so that when I am eligible to trade on the stock market I will have an abundant amount of money to trade with etc. There are so many forms of investments. Investing proves to yourself that you are serious. Investing is important. It takes you to the next level. Every successful investment will take you a step closer to your major life goal.

10 – Ten percent of all of my profits are for me and my daily expenditure, for example food and drink. I don't use all of this usually. I believe that it is important to have some money for yourself so that you can treat yourself after each major and minor achievement.

Failing to Plan Is Planning to Fail

I've noticed that failing to plan is planning to fail. I am not quite certain who said that quote first although he/she is spot on as it still applies today. When I do not plan out my day, I waste so much time, it's almost unbelievable. When you are an entrepreneur, you are your own boss, meaning; the only person that has the authority to hold you accountable for your actions is you, therefore, it is easy to waste time as nobody will come after you making sure you get the work done. You either do it for yourself or you don't do it at all. You most certainly WILL waste time if you do not plan out your day. So I would strongly advise planning each day out. As Jim Rohn says, "Don't start your day until you've finished it." Of course you cannot plan it out second by second and expect it to go exactly to plan but you can plan it hour by hour or half hour by half hour. Planning your days out with a goal in mind for each day, week, month and year will keep you in the correct mind set which you unquestionably need to fulfil your goals. Your daily plans should lead you to the fulfilment of your daily, weekly, monthly and yearly goals. Working on something every day will keep you focused and motivated. Self-motivation grows overtime from within. Getting serious with yourself is like a fertiliser for your self-motivation. Making daily plans shows that you are serious.

Self-belief and Self-confidence

I've noticed the undoubtable importance of self-belief and self-confidence. Those two qualities alone have truly changed my life. When I manifested the belief in my ability to achieve goals, every day became full of energy, enthusiasm and productivity. *People believe in people who believe in themselves.* That is a fact. You will not believe what someone says, no matter how logically he or she explains their motion, if they do not show a belief in it themselves. If someone is merely reciting a script with no emotion or belief in what they are saying, they are not likely to hold onto your attention. When a salesperson truly believes in the product during his/her pitch, you can't help but absorb some of that belief.

Self-education

I've noticed that the saying, 'the more you learn, the more you can earn', is an absolute fact.

Before I began educating myself, I would rarely ever make a sale or receive money. A few months into my self-education and I was making at least six sales every week. Education pays so invest in your knowledge. Reading this book is a great start.

With Darkness Comes Light

I've noticed that the best of times and the biggest opportunities have come from my greatest hardships and the lowest moments in my life. This helps me appreciate my hardships as I know with confidence that something great will come out of them. Life is most certainly comparable to a rollercoaster when we take a step back and observe it. Every dip will lead into the next high.

Dwelling Is Destructive

I've noticed that dwelling on anything, whether it is positive or negative, does not serve you. Dwelling on something implies that you are thinking about it and not only that but you are also *overthinking* about it. This will never be good for you. Dwelling on something from the past is unexplainable and dwelling on something which is in the future is unnecessary. There is no need to dwell on anything. Visualising my goals is the closest that I allow myself to get to dwell on something.

Live In the Moment

I've noticed that the most productive way for me to live my life has been living in the moment and allowing everything that happens to happen. When we resist thoughts, situations etc. we merely give them more control, as our thoughts are powerful especially when there is a feeling driving them. When a feeling is driving them, it is not only our head that is giving the thought power but our heart is also giving the thought power. Staying present has truly served me. It keeps me focused.

We Reap What We've Sown

I've noticed that *our inputs are a direct link to our outputs.* Think of your mind as a pancake mixture. If you put in bad quality ingredients or the wrong ingredients, you cannot expect a good final product. Only the correct ingredients and the right timing will give us the pancakes, results, which we want. Think about that last sentence.

We Become What We Believe We Are

I've noticed that our lives are a physical manifestation of our *subconscious* beliefs. When we consciously believe/think that we are wealthy and have an abundance of cash although our subconscious mind believes and knows that we owe people money and we lack cash, we will attract and manifest our subconscious beliefs. We reprogram our subconscious mind to believing that we have an abundance of wealth and energy. This can be done via a shift in our paradigms. Reciting affirmations aloud with conviction and feeling every day is a tried and tested method of shifting our paradigms. Our paradigms are basically our subconscious beliefs. They are said to having been programmed throughout our first seven years. By the age of seven, our paradigms have been programmed by our outer environment – what we have been told, what we have seen, what we have heard etc. Shift your paradigms.

Swapping Time for Money Limits Income

I've noticed that formal education will confine you to swapping your time for money whereas self-education allows you the freedom to swap your value for money by creating streams of passive income. We must create value, for example a book, and then swap that for money. That way, even ten years from when you first started selling the book, you can still get paid for it as it is VALUABLE. Value pays. As long as you are answering to someone, you will never have true freedom. I've noticed that people only treat us how we allow them to. We only live with what we settle for. If we only swap our time for money, we are strongly limited by how much we can earn as we only have so much time! Create value and let that pay you.

Everyone Thinks They're Right

I've noticed that most everyone thinks that they are fair and correct no matter how logically wrong or delusional they may truly be. Everyone thinks that they are right. We are better off allowing someone to think that they are correct rather than opening up an argument with them. As I've mentioned previously, arguments are never won. We must be careful and make sure to not hurt people's pride and ego. Hurting someone's ego is a direct link to them resenting you. When somebody wants to think that they are correct, let them. It is no loss to you if they stubbornly believe that they are correct. Just allow it and stay present.

Meditation Matters

I've noticed just how beneficial meditation can be when practiced regularly. I meditate for at least ten minutes every single day. It has allowed me to become much calmer and much more peaceful. I am now less likely to lose my temper and I have become more accepting. I have now ranked my personal happiness at the top of my list of priorities. Meditating daily for the past few months has definitely multiplied my ability to focus on tasks and to stay focused for longer. My focus is much stronger now. Now, I can plan and execute with ease. We are all fully capable executing *what we have planned.* Planning is still the key! Consistent meditation has truly opened my mind. I am slower to discard ideas. This has allowed me to embrace and emit my creativity. I have become more able to express myself and my feelings. I am easier to talk to now as I am more open to other people's views and perspectives. I have also gained a huge volume of respect for nature. I notice how my appreciation for nature has grown greatly. Nature has so much to offer. It is priceless. Meditation has been scientifically proven to eliminate and/or at least dramatically decrease levels of anxiety when practiced for as little as eight weeks at a rate of ten minutes per day. Include meditation in your daily routine.

Yoga? YES

Practicing yoga daily has also helped me greatly in living a happy and energetic lifestyle. I usually go through my yoga routine in the morning about an hour after I wake up. I find this to be the perfect time for me as my muscles are not tired anymore and a good stretch is truly needed. Nowadays I can't go through my day without performing a yoga routine. I become very lazy and I have the urge to sit around and do nothing when I skip my morning yoga routine. It doesn't take much for my body to feel a good stretch. Even after just a fifteen minute yoga session, I can feel my energy levels beginning to rejuvenate. Yoga keeps me flexible and fit. It also helps my mind to clear itself. It allows me to release any stress within my mind and/or my body. I find yoga to be exceptionally enjoyable. I have lots of fun during my short sessions. If you want to find me at 7:30am, I am most likely in the cobra position on the beige carpets of my sitting room. My favourite 'pose' in my usual routine is definitely the head stand. Headstands are amazing. They help us to circulate blood around our bodies. After a headstand, I can truly feel a rush of energy drowning my body. Even just a thirty second headstand can greatly increase my energy levels for the rest of the day. Headstands are a great addition to any yoga routine.

Fashion

I've noticed how the fashion culture in Ireland is slowly growing. More and more people are gaining interests in global fashion trends. Nowadays, more people are rejecting the idea of everyone wearing the same clothes and having the same style. People are beginning to have more respect for exclusive clothes. They want to express themselves through the clothes that they are wearing. Many people are starting to customise their clothes themselves so that it is a true one-of-a-kind piece that they will never see someone else wearing. The fashion industry in Ireland, quite like the music industry, is tremendously desiccated and quite bare. Ireland is not known for its fashion yet. However, I must say, we most certainly have some spectacular designers. I saw some of the pieces designed by the graduates of NCAD in the summer of 2017. They were phenomenal. I predict that our fashion industry will take off in the next decade. There is so much talent here in Ireland.

Appearance

I've noticed that the more you create, the more people recognise you. I've been posting content consistently for around two years now and I'm constantly stopped for chats or photos wherever I go. Most people don't *really* do anything at all. As soon as you start *consistently* doing something out of the ordinary, you *will* attract attention. People *will* know who you are. They will stare and they will take pictures and videos of you without you even knowing! This behaviour can be annoying at first although I've learned to think about it from their point of view. It's weird though. I'm not famous or hard to talk to. I reply to 99% of my messages but people love hype so much that they will create hype where there is none. If you see me in public, say 'hello', I'm a human like the rest of us. We are all one.

With that being said, I would always recommend keeping your appearance in good condition. You never know who you may meet and your appearance will forever be your first impression. I'm not saying to wear heaps of makeup and dress up in really expensive designer clothes everywhere you go. I'm saying, stay clean and fresh. Simple as. No need to be fancy, just stay clean and fresh. That applies to your body and your clothes. Your appearance is most definitely your first impression.

FORMAL EDUCATION CAN MAKE YOU A **LIVING**,

SELF EDUCATION CAN MAKE YOU A *FORTUNE*. ~ Jim Rohn

"college won't save you"

Chapter 4

WHITE BRICK WALLS

'Inspired By the Boy Who Desired Freedom'
The Power of Self-Education, Meditation & Being a Student.

We all have a burning desire. Mine happens to be unconditional freedom. Physical freedom, mental freedom, spiritual freedom, creative freedom, financial freedom etc. I desire a life of unconditional freedom. This desire stemmed partly from my experience of formal education, secondary school.

Before we dive too deep into this chapter, let me clarify; I am neither anti–school nor anti–education. I am quite the opposite in fact. This chapter merely outlines part of my experience in school and my views on the schooling system. If my opinions and/or ideas offend you, I am glad that I got you thinking. As Jim Rohn says, "Be a student, not a follower." In other words, make up your own mind on this subject. Do not take anyone's opinion as your own – including mine - unless you have pondered the opinion for yourself and truly agree with it.

When I first started secondary school, I loved it. I had learned from my mistakes of primary school. I was quite popular in primary school, although, near the end of my days there, I noticed an adjustment in my priorities which caused me to lose basically all of my friends. I was more focused on my future than I was on, 'who won the match last night' or 'the concert being played this summer'. I spent hours every day on my personal growth and development in terms of understanding the law of attraction and how to practice it effectively. Being 11, of course none of my peers cared to ponder such ideas or would even begin to understand me if I had tried to explain them. I noticed how my 'friends' were losing interest in me and at the time I wasn't too concerned. I had already lost interest in the people whom I used to call my 'best friends'. I didn't enjoy their company and their shallow conversations anymore. My mind was possibly overdeveloped for my age although looking back, I can't complain as it gave me quite a head start for secondary school.

During the summer before entering my first year of secondary school, I spent hours and hours researching and experimenting dozens and dozens of conversational techniques and psychologically proven ways to make people like you. It may sound sad but I wanted friends. *I wanted to be popular.* I also wanted to see if everything that I had been vigorously learning about would actually work for me.

The following is a basic version of my experience in and my feelings towards secondary school. Again, my views are taken solely from my personal story. Be a student not a follower.

By the second week of 'First Year', I knew at least 75% of the students in my school. I felt like a master networker. I was friendly with many of the older students as well as those my own age. However, soon enough, I got cocky and lost my spark. My ego kicked in. I began to assume that people would like me without applying the techniques that I had learned. They didn't like me; they liked how I treated them. I made them feel important, as I was told to do although I probably over did it.

Those techniques changed me. I wasn't being myself anymore. I was a made up character; 'DTMD'.

At that time, I performed magic. I had a whole catalogue of card tricks and one illusion with my ring. You could always find a deck of cards in my pocket. I would perform for at least twenty people every day. When I performed, I would embrace this 'better version of myself' who I named 'DTMD'. I would become very conscious and present while performing and my mind was working so speedily. I would be recalling the advice I had heard in a YouTube video five months ago and remembering a 'key card' lying three positions above the spectator's chosen card at the same time. When I reflect on those days, I don't know how I remembered everything. That wasn't me though. That was me *trying* to be my best version. I have since learned that our true self is more than enough. *We need not seek anything outside of ourselves as all that we need is within.*

The moral of that little story is; I spent so much time trying to get other people interested in me that *I* wasn't even interested in me. As Dale Carnegie rightly said, '*You can make more friends in two months by becoming interested in other people than you can in two years by trying to get other people interested in you.*" That quote is the absolute truth.

I was a complete sell out with a few hundred acquaintances who I called 'friends'. I didn't want to admit this to myself because I didn't know any different and of course at the age of 12 I was afraid of criticism and change.

During the summer of 'First Year', I released the first Joker Clothing™ pieces and published pictures from the photoshoots on Facebook and Instagram. I was a different person after that summer and everyone treated me differently. I came back to school in late august and by the end of the first day; I saw how everyone had 'switched up'. I felt like I couldn't trust anyone anymore just from the vibes that I got. With that being said, I continued to force the few 'friendships' that I had until January/February. That's when I started networking properly. I met so many new, amazing people from December onwards living all over the world. I would spend up to four hours every day after school talking to new people over skype. I made friends with so many celebrities and none of them acted big headed or stuck up.

There was a stage in 'Second Year' where a certain rapper released a new album and while everyone in school was listening to his album and talking about him, I was listening to the dude's voice over skype and talking *to him*.

I let go of basically all of my secondary school 'friends' by the end of that school year. I also let go of my motivation to finish school that year. I felt like my time was being wasted while in school, especially when certain teachers would consistently not show up to class or not stay for the full forty minutes. Also, the celebrities that I was talking to were telling me how they would drop out if they were me. This of course had an influence on my mind set. That school year was my worst. However, it taught me so much. It also gave me a whole new drive. I knew that the only way for me to become free from school would be for me to become extremely successful. That would be the only plausible way. That summer, I dropped my first real collection under Joker Clothing™. The #DoingMe collection. That collection was then mass produced and made me my first real money. This made my third year of secondary school even harder.

When people don't see it for themselves, they won't see it for you.

Over the summer, I worked on myself. I built myself. In January of 'Third Year', I found myself and my purpose. I realised my end goal; unconditional freedom. I proceeded to create a plan of action to get me there.

HOW TO GET THROUGH SCHOOL

Be yourself. Do you. This applies to all situations. When we are not being our true selves, of course we will feel uncomfortable and out of place. *We feel out of place because our body is in school but our soul is in someplace else.* We cannot feel comfortable somewhere when we are not fully there. We will feel comfortable, accepted, in place, happy and free when we are;

1. In alignment with our true self (being ourselves).

2. Aware of our inner body.

Inner body awareness keeps us present and when we are present, we have no worries. There is nothing to worry about in the 'now' (more on this topic in chapter 2).

I am sure that some of you are in the same or a similar situation like I was in during my three years of secondary school. To you, I say this; 'keep on going. Do not stop following your dreams for ANYBODY. Realise that the only person who can take you where you want to go is the best version of yourself, so work on yourself harder than you work on anything else. Spend more time on the development of yourself than you do on anything else. You're worth it. Keep on educating yourself. Save as much money as you can while you're young. You'll thank yourself for that later. Keep strict disciplines. Wake up early – the best time is sunrise but ease your way into waking up that early, baby steps are proven to provide longer lasting results – and assign yourself tasks to complete, *even if you do not have an end goal yet.* Do something. Learn as much as you can and take action. Create every day. Write a poem or a song. Learn how to draw a perfect eye from YouTube. Better your crafts in some way every single day. Design a collection of clothes for next summer. Learn tips and tricks on how to take the perfect photo and/or video. Learn a skill or make a good. Anything is better than nothing, no matter how small it may seem. When you are constantly keeping yourself busy and doing something productive that you enjoy, you will begin to feel better about yourself. You will believe in yourself more and love yourself more. DO SOMETHING EVERY DAY.'

BREAK THE WALLS

When we rely on a system we can become complacent. We get comfortable. We see the 'safety net' and live life on autopilot. *Autopilot can only bring us so far.* My definition of a 'safety net' in this context is; 'something that we can tolerate although we know that it is not our ultimate life purpose.' Some people call it a 'plan B'. Many people see social welfare as their safety net. They allow themselves to relax through the times when work could and should have been done. Relying on getting a day job when we leave school – if we do not get into the right college course – is a safety net. You either do it or you don't. There's a simple formula to get into a college.

Either follow it to the letter and get in or don't try at all. There's no point in wasting your time, pretending that you are trying to get in and then not actually following the steps or putting in the work and then settling for minimum wage in your local grocery store. This is where definiteness of purpose comes in. If you want something, go and get it. Formulas are made to work when followed.

I must say this; 'if you are happy then keep doing you, happiness is the number one priority. This is for the complainers and those of us who want more.'

The pay check to pay check lifestyle will not allow you the freedom that you deserve. If you want true freedom, you'll have to become your own boss.

You will have to break free of the walls that are holding you inside this box. Get outside the box. Think outside the box. Be outside the box. Break those white brick walls. You can do this by learning what school won't teach you. Learn about the seven hermetic principles. Understand and practice the '48 Laws of Power'. To really break the walls, you must understand what the walls are. They are the limitations you were brought up to believe in. Think of it like this; if Michael Jordan believed that he wasn't able to shoot a basket successfully would he ever try? If you believed that you couldn't swim would you jump into the ocean? We are only limited by our beliefs. They are the white brick walls. From my time in school, the walls I've seen being built around myself and my classmates include the following:

o You have to do well in school.
o Rich people are all crooks and corrupt.
o Money is hard to acquire.
o You can only swap your time for money.
o Exam results define your future.
o You need to go to college to earn lots of money.
o Money is evil.
o Hard work is the only way to get anything.
o Everyone is out to get you.
o People's opinions of you matter.
o We are limited beings.
o Not all of us can live happily together.
o We must obey our elders religiously.
o Age is a restriction to living your life.

Break the walls and live.

EDUCATE YOURSELF

Education is so important. It is what differentiates you from everyone else. The average person reads between four and six books every year. Keep in mind that these figures are inflated by avid readers and the books in question are usually fictional and unproductive. I'm going to make a generous estimate by saying, 'The average person reads 1 personal development book in their life and doesn't finish or apply it'. Most don't read one at all! Did you know that there is a book dedicated to the in depth explanation on how to acquire literally any position you desire? There are books that will teach you how to make friends, how to make money, how to make dinner, how to get the job that you want, how to make new habits and quit old ones, how to heal yourself, how to travel with ease in any country etc. There is literally a book explaining EVERYTHING and most people still complain about those things without even trying to learn how to solve them. If you want more money, learn how to make more. Buy a book, take some notes and take action. *Invest in the right book and it will repay the largest profits.* Knowledge is your greatest asset. As they say, 'The more you learn, the more you can earn.' My favourite definition of an educated person is as follows; 'an educated person is one who is capable of acquiring what he or she desires without violating the rights of others.'

LACKING CONCENTRATION?

Meditation has been scientifically proven to improve concentration, focus and memory. It has truly worked wonders in my life. I have reaped the benefits of daily meditation. Meditation helped me to break out of the white brick walls. *When we focus on our desired destination, not the journey, roadblocks and walls are no longer in the picture.* Meditation will help you to get clear on your goals. We must know where we are trying to go before we can expect to get there!

It can be hard to stay focused when our friends want to bring us to parties and spend time with them. There are so many distractions. We can lose track of whose life we are really living at times. We can find ourselves living for everyone around us rather than living for ourselves. If we want to fulfil our daily, weekly, monthly and yearly goals then we must put them at the top of our list of priorities. There is no point setting a goal but choosing to waste six hours of everyday with your best friend instead of spending that time on your goals. When we are serious about our goals, we put them over everything.

Proper practices of the breathing techniques from chapter two are forms of meditation. These will keep you relaxed and focused throughout the day. They will also speed up your learning process. The faster you learn (relevant information), the faster you can earn. Here's one piece of relevant information from Jim Rohn that you *need to know* on the topic of accumulating riches; *we are paid for the value we bring, not our time. If we were payed for our time, we could just play games all day and collect our pay checks every month.* With this in mind, *is it possible to become twice as valuable and earn twice as much? Of course!*

Jim Rohn always advises his students to *work harder on themselves than they do on their job.* This way, they will become more valuable as people and not have to give as much time away. They swap their value for money instead of their time. Yes, it takes time to become more valuable but that time is only spent once and the value acquired lasts forever.

IN SCHOOL WE SHOULD…

In school we should learn how to think not what to think. We should learn the art of application not theory. We should learn how to create jobs not how to fill them. We should learn how to trade stocks not how to write emails. We should learn how to talk to people not how to write letters. We should learn how to make others feel important not how to make others feel inferior. We should learn how to be disciplined not how to avoid confrontation. We should learn how to dream big not how to settle.

In school we should be educated not taught.

YOUR GRADES DO NOT DEFINE YOU

Many people are under the false impression that they are not capable of acquiring the life which they desire as their grades from school were not high enough. They think that they cannot be ambitious as the letter after each subject on their report card does not read 'A'. For those people I say this; 'YOU ARE WORTH MORE THAN A LETTER. The results we get in an exam are not a reflection of who we are or what we are capable of.'

At the end of every school year, overly stressed students are seen in every café, library, bedroom and kitchen trying to cram those final few details into their short term memory. *What's the purpose?* They will usually tell you that they want to go to a good college – to do more stressful 'work' with no guarantees of satisfaction. When they're asked why they are going to college, they will usually explain how they need that college course to get the job that they want. So they will sacrifice years of their happiness, time, opportunities and inner peace for a job. This job must be amazing. It must bring them true joy and freedom. I would sacrifice all of the above for a job that allowed me unconditional freedom! They proceed to fill you in on this mysterious, dream job and why they want it so badly. They'll usually tell you that it pays well. However, the job is on their boss' terms, they must answer to their boss. They have to be there on time and do what they are told to do. They have set holidays and a few extra sick days. They are not in charge of their own income. They must swap their time for money, meaning that while they are not working, they will not be getting payed. Why would

they sacrifice so much for yet another sacrifice? A job on those terms is most definitely a sacrifice.

Their whole life is answering to other people and making others happy. In school they hand in their homework when their teacher asks them to. They do what the teacher tells them to do in class. Then they do the same in college. Then they do the same in work. Who cares about money? Why are most people so ruled by money? Those same people will call out successful entrepreneurs and say that they are driven by money which is not at all true 99% of the time.

If you dedicate your whole life solely to making money, doesn't that make *you* money driven?

Whereas, if you dedicate your whole life solely to making jobs for others, doesn't that make you an honourable person? Of course successful entrepreneurs are rich, they deserve their money. They live for the betterment of their community not the betterment of their bank account, that's merely a by-product of the work that they undertake.

Money is merely an energy that you can attract. They don't need to spend more than ten years in formal education to get a degree, to get a job, to get money. They don't have to. That's not the only way to make money and that most certainly will not bring them happiness. If they only spent one year educating themselves on the seven hermetic principles and the laws of the universe AND APPLIED THAT KNOWLEDGE, they would be much happier, healthier, calmer, more relaxed, more accepting and much wealthier. As Ralph Smart says, 'Money is energy that is why it is called currency'. *Wealth is purely a state of mind.* Gary Vaynerchuk, my current favourite entrepreneur and speaker, never did well in school. He is open about his unsuccessful formal education. What makes him different from most others who do not perform well academically is that he did not use his school grades as a petty excuse to not follow his dreams. He had set a standard for himself and he was not going to stop working until he had acquired that standard for his life. He had a desire, an end goal. He made definite decisions and yes, of course he made some wrong decisions but he allowed them, learned from them and moved on. He didn't have time to be focusing on his losses and failures. He was way too focused on getting to where he wanted to be and nothing could stop him. He worked on his dream without a day's holiday for over 13 years. No exceptions, no excuses. He put in the work. He made them calls. He created the content. He deserves all of his success. People still call him corrupt just because he chose his own route of which to take on his path through life. Most people have a subconscious hatred towards successful and/or rich people. Even those born into wealthy families have to work both hard and smart every day to achieve. *When our money is low, we must spend our time instead.* Your grades do not define you, your character does. Live on your own terms.

SUCCESS HAS NO AGE

Whether you're ten years old, twenty years old, thirty years old, forty years old, fifty years old, sixty years old, seventy years old, eighty years old, ninety years old or past your hundredth year, we all have quite a few advantages in common. No matter where you live in the world, no matter what gender you are, no matter what sexuality you class yourself as, no matter what people think of you, we all share common controls. The following is Ruben Chavez's list of 'Things you can control':

o   Your beliefs

- o Your attitude
- o Your thoughts
- o Your perspective
- o How honest you are
- o Who your friends are
- o What books you read
- o How often you exercise
- o The type of food you eat
- o How many risks you take
- o How kind you are to others
- o How you interpret situations
- o How kind you are to yourself
- o How you express your feelings
- o How often you say, 'I love you'
- o How often you say, 'thank you'
- o Whether or not you ask for help
- o How often you practice gratitude
- o How many times you smile today
- o How you spend/invest you money
- o The amount of effort you put forth
- o How much time you spend worrying
- o How often you think about your past
- o Whether or not you judge other people
- o How much you appreciate what you have
- o Whether or not you try again after a setback

When we consider this list, we realise that we have no reason to complain. No matter what our outer circumstances are saying, we can still smile and make the best out of it. Revise this list of controls. We are more powerful than we think.

"depressed or in need of deep rest?"*

*Ralph Smart

Chapter 5

DEEPREST

'Inspired By the Boy Who Learned to Love Living'
The Power of Happiness, Allowing, Sleep and Visualisation.

HOW TO BE HAPPY

The most common, underlying topic of queries that I read in my messages all recount to happiness. We must recognise that happiness is a choice. It is a fact that simply smiling for sixty seconds will make us happier. Spare a minute to gaze out of the window and just smile.

A common misunderstanding is that money brings us happiness. This is not true for all people and when it is true we must remember, *lasting happiness can only come from within.* Nevertheless, what *is* the truth for *all* people is the following phrase; 'happiness brings money' – as they are energetic matches with each other. The principle of correspondence states, as within, so without. This means that the energies we feel on the inside, in this case happiness, will manifest into the physical/outer world. When we are happy, we are not worrying, we are care free. We are expecting good things to happen to us. We are fearless. This means that we will manifest these energies into the physical world. This can be in the form of many things, subject to the person, for me however, this is usually in the form of money. When I'm having a remarkably happy day, I'll get a few notifications on my phone stating how much money just lodged into my account. It's incredible! *In our pursuit of happiness, we must think of happiness in terms of energy.*

This is the basics of a universal law also. The law of attraction – as made popular by the inspiring book titled, 'The Secret' by Rhonda Byrne – is basically the principle of correspondence. Rhonda explains this principle in immense detail. Reading her book puts a smile on my face every time so I would definitely recommend giving it a read, after you finish this one of course!

Happiness emanates from many different sources. For some people, it can be from playing sports or from playing video games. However for others, it might only come from spending time with friends and/or family. My Mother loves being outdoors. She is more than happy to be gardening from dawn until dusk as long as she's outside in nature and has her own space and resources to create. However, this wouldn't appeal to everyone as our likes and dislikes are all different. I could sit on a beach and stare at the waves all day. I could also sit in my room sketching or writing all day. *I enjoy creating and consuming art.* That brings me happiness. In conclusion, to be happy, we must know what makes us happy. This will make life so much easier for you. Find the piece of paper you used in chapter one and turn it over to the blank side. Like before, draw a line straight down the middle of the sheet of paper. Title the left column 'What Brings Me Energy' and title the left column 'What Drains My Energy'. As you're reading this, I want you to think of at least twenty entries for each of the columns. These entries can consist of names of people, names of places, types of music, names of films, certain circumstances, types of videos, specific actions, apps, postures/poses, material items, foods, drinks, smells, feelings, particular sights, particular sounds, types of lighting etc. Beside each entry, write the number of times you practice the entry per week.

Again, I'll include some of mine below:

What Brings Me Energy?

Meditation [7 – 10]

Yoga [7 – 10]

Skating [10 – 15]

Recording Videos [2 – 7]

Writing Instagram Captions [5 –7]

Eating Fruits [7]

Dancing [5 – 7]

Singing [5 –7]

Creating [20 – 25]

Giving Unrepayable Value [10 – 25]

What Drains My Energy?

Bass Heavy Music [3 – 7]

Consciously Wasting Time [7]

Conversing With Complainers [1 – 3]

Eating Non Vegan Foods [7] – I will most likely embrace the vegan lifestyle by the time you read this.

Being In Crowds/Big Groups of People [2 – 5]

Overindulging In Material Items [3 – 10]

Failing To Plan [0 – 2]

Drinking Fizzy Drinks [0 – 3]

Overthinking [0 – 5]

Sleeping For Too Long [0 – 2]

These lists are gold. You should read over your lists every day. There is so much value in the two lists that you've just created. They will literally change your life. Now you know what gives you energy – what makes you happy – and what drains your energy – what reduces your happiness. Think of it like this, when positivity is absent, the only thing else to take its place is negativity. *When we are not proactively creating circumstances that will bring us underlying happiness and positivity into our lives, we cannot be in shock when underlying sadness and negativity comes to fill the vacancy.*

Repeat this exercise every Sunday before you go to sleep. Review and analyse your week and compare it to the week before. Make a conscious effort to increase the figures after the entries in your left column and decrease the figures after the entries in the right column. This will prove to yourself that you are serious about your happiness. That alone will put a smile on your face. The majority of people will do more of what drains their energy per week than what gives them energy. No wonder they complain all the time. Complaining takes zero effort. Anyone can complain. Those who create instead of complain are the ones who have energy, not that you can't see it in their faces already! 'OFTEN WHEN WE PRETEND TO BE HAPPY OUR MIND AND BODY BELIEVES US'. Choose happiness today and every other day. Someone, somewhere on this planet is having the best day of their life today, join them!

HOW TO FORGET FEAR

Fear is the most common cause of failure. Napoleon Hill addresses the six most commonly found fears among humans in his extraordinary bestseller entitled, 'Think and Grow Rich'. Here they are in order taken from the Epilogue of 'Think and Grow Rich':

'The fear of POVERTY (at the heart of most people's worries)

The fear of CRITICISM

The fear of ILL HEALTH

The fear of LOSS OF LOVE OF SOMEONE

The fear of OLD AGE

The fear of DEATH'

Do you recognise any or all of these fears within you? Fear is not necessary. It blocks us from happiness and positivity and leads us to sadness and negativity. When I first read the above fears, I spent a week in search of them. I lived through my normal schedules although each morning I wrote out the six fears on a piece of paper in an effort to remember them throughout the day and be conscious of them at all times. It worked. However, I did not need seven days. By the end of the first day, I had already recognised all six fears. We must understand that fears can be conscious *and* subconscious. Our conscious fears accommodate our thoughts. These, we can eliminate in seconds by simply bringing attention to them. Do not give them energy, just view them. View them as neutral thoughts. No thoughts are universally positive and/or are universally negative. We choose whether a thought is positive or negative. Therefore, we can view these thoughts and allow them to move on. I like to think of it as confronting our thoughts. When we confront our thoughts, they get intimidated and move on, they run away from confrontation. Viewing our thoughts is how we confront them. Recognise and acknowledge the thought and allow it. Do not resist it as that will give it energy and make it more powerful. As Ralph Smart says, 'resistance only makes stronger'. We must allow. Whether we agree with the thought and/or fear or not, we must allow it to exist just as we allow the breeze to blow. Fear will always exist in our minds. Our minds will always be afraid of the unknown, that's just human nature – from what I've experienced. However, fear does not live in the now. The same way that worry does not exist in the now. Things change every moment. We mustn't be afraid of the past as we cannot change it. We mustn't fear the future as it does not yet exist. Why would we fear something which does not even exist? That idea alone sounds absurd when we bring attention to it although our minds have been practicing that idea for as long as we've been able to think!

HOW TO KILL THE WORRYING HABIT

Why do we worry? We worry for many different reasons. Overthinking and overanalysing leads to worrying. When we take everything personally we become sensitive to worry. When we allow negativity to rule our day we begin to worry. When we are attached to our past we become victims of worry. Regret leads to worry. When we resist we attract worry. When we want to leave the present moment we can become worried. When we overindulge in stimulants – caffeine, alcohol, narcotics etc. we become worried. When we force situations, relationships, circumstances, beliefs etc. we will worry. Fear will always lead to worry. Rumination leads to worry. When we forget what makes us happy we can begin to acquire the worrying habit – don't lose your sheet!

HOW TO SLEEP BETTER

Sleep is very important. The more you create, the more you'll come to realise this fact. Effective sleep reenergises us and keeps our bodies functioning efficiently. The lack of sleep can lead to obesity. However, getting the correct hours of sleep improves your hormones. Correct sleep is even known to relieving stress. Even your immune system is improved as your sleep is improved. Good sleep helps your body to fight off sicknesses. Recent studies have shown that those who sleep seven hours, or less, per night are more likely to catch a cold than those who sleep eight hours or more per night. Sleeping well will increase your learning ability, capacity and speed. Studies show that more data is remembered when we learn right before a good night's sleep than when we learn during the day. Good sleep has even been found to decrease your chances of developing depression. It has been estimated that 90% of patients who suffer from diagnosed depression also acquire a form of sleep apnea. If you're trying to lose weight, focus instead on getting the correct amount sleep. People who sleep for longer naturally eat less. Better sleep has been proven to help us understand others and social ques. Sleep will improve your physical and athletic performance. Sleep occupies up to a third of your life, why wouldn't you do it properly?

Now that you know why sleeping is so important and beneficial, here are a few tips to get a better night's sleep:

1. Use Blackout Curtains – our sleeping hormone, melatonin, is raised when the sun sets to signal our bodies that it is time to rest. Unnatural lighting confuses this hormone. Make your room pitch black. By fully blacking out your room, you will notice a huge increase in the quality of sleep and you will fall asleep quicker and more easily. All sorts of lit up screens confuse your melatonin hormones. Yes, this includes your phone too!

2. Create a Sleep Routine – this can be anything. For example; brush your teeth, plan out tomorrow, read a book for ten minutes and read over your goals then go straight to sleep. This routine will program your body to fall asleep after reading over your goals every night. Habits work. You will find yourself falling asleep with great ease.

3. Only Sleep in Your Bed – again, this will become a habit and your body will expect to sleep when you hit your bed. Refrain from relaxing or spending any time on your bed. Only be on your bed when you are going through your routine and when you are sleeping.

4. Sleep With a Pillow Between/Underneath Your Legs – I have found this to be greatly beneficial in my personal practice. It has without a doubt improved my posture and maintained the alignment in my spine, as it is said to. I used to have, what felt like, a slightly curved spine. This would be quite agonising throughout the day. Sleeping with a pillow

between or underneath my legs has definitely eased my spinal pains. It straightened up my back AND helps me fall asleep faster as it is super comfortable!

5. Take Short Naps – 20 to 30 minute naps lower your cortisol levels and are very healthy for your body. They will rejuvenate your energy levels and have been proven to increase productivity levels.

Those five tips, when followed correctly, should allow you some better quality sleep and more productive days. *Quality sleep combined with quality goals and quality daily practice will bring quality results.* Give those five suggestions above a test for yourself. See how well you can sleep tonight.

THE BETTER YOU SLEEP, THE BETTER YOU WAKE. The recommended sleep duration is no less than seven hours and no more than nine hours. Keep this in mind when scheduling your sleep cycle.

HOW TO LUCID DREAM

Lucid dreaming is the fascinating state of awareness within a dream. We are lucid dreaming when we are aware that we are dreaming while we are in a dream. When we are in this state, we can control our dreams. We can do whatever we want and go wherever we want. When put to productive use, lucid dreaming can be utilised as a powerful form of visualisation. We can accomplish all of our goals in our lucid dream. This can help us understand how we *will* feel once we accomplish each goal in real life. This is priceless information. We can use the law of attraction effectively once we know which feelings will attract what we want. It's also a magnificent platform of which you can face your fears.

1. Start a Dream Journal – every morning before you get on with your day, write down as many details as you can remember from your dreams. This will help and encourage you to remember and be aware of your dreams.

2. Set an Alarm for 6 Hours after Going to Bed – this is when you enter your longest REM sleep cycle. In your rapid eye movement – REM – cycle your mind is closer to alert wakefulness so the possibility to realise that you are dreaming and gain control of your dream rises. You are more likely to enter a lucid dream in this sleep cycle than any other.

3. Wake Up With the Alarm – when your alarm goes off, after six hours, wake up and use the bathroom if needed. Take note of any dreams in your journal.

4. Imagine Your Lucid Dream – lay back down in your bed and imagine what you would do and where you would go in your lucid dream. Visualise yourself performing these actions repeatedly.

5. Affirm Your Lucid Dream – before you go back to sleep to enter your lucid dream, affirm to yourself that you will lucid dream by means of repeating in your mind, 'I am lucid dreaming' for a few minutes. This will help your subconscious mind believe that you can and will lucid dream.

6. Sleep – now, go to sleep as you usually would. If you do not lucid dream on your first attempt, do not worry. It took me until my fourth day trying to finally lucid dream. No matter the result of the night, record your results in the dream journal.

Now that you know how to lucid dream, you must learn how to remain in your dream. Usually during our first experience, we get too excited and wake ourselves up by accident. We must make an effort to stay relatively calm and refrain from rushing into anything. Embrace the awareness of your surroundings before you go off, living life to the fullest or you may end up back in the real world sooner than expected. Observe your surroundings by engaging all of your senses. Touch what you see in your dream. Become very present in your dream to solidify the scene in your mind. One thing that I do when I begin to lose awareness is rubbing my hands together. I rub my hands together, in the dream not in real life, and it brings me back into the moment. Engaging our senses will always bring us back into the present moment. Always remember, practice makes perfect. Keep on attempting to lucid dream and you will eventually get it right. Consistent practice is definitely needed.

HOW TO VISUALISE

Visualisation is a very beneficial part of the manifesting process. It is a technique which can be used to understand how we will feel when we acquire what we desire. For example, if someone wants more money, they can visualise receiving a cheque in the mail or having a few extra thousand euro in their bank account. Our minds don't know what is real and what is not unless we consciously decide that something is real or fake – just like right and wrong. When we program our minds to believe that we will receive more money every day, our minds will expect it and you will find yourself in new situations where acquiring money is possible. For example; you may meet a new client. Do not expect the money to just be handed to you. We usually attract the opportunities that will enable us to acquire what we want. With repetition, we will engrave into our minds that we will receive more money today and every day. Every time you visualise successfully, that will become more believable to both your conscious and subconscious mind. You do not need to visualise for hours every day, some gurus recommend between 1 and 3 minutes of visualisation per day and other gurus recommend 15 – 20 seconds per time at least five times a day.

STEPS TO VISUALISING:

1. Get Clear about Our Intention – make a definite decision on what you want to manifest. Know what you want. Know why you are visualising. What are you trying to achieve by visualising?

2. Know How It Would Feel – know how you would feel when you achieve your intention from the first step. Bring strong awareness to these feelings. They will be the determining factor of whether or not you end up manifesting what you are visualising.

3. Close Your Eyes – close your eyes and focus on the feeling. Do not force images to be pressed into your brain. Images will come from focusing on the

feeling. When we force an image to show up, it is not clear enough to be believable. Instead, focus on the feelings of having what you desire already. Hold onto these feelings and allow any images or colours or shapes that enter your mind to stay. Do not resist or dwell on them. That would be resisting what you desire. Put all of your thoughts and feelings towards what you desire. Images will come back to you. Allow them, no matter what they are. It's more about our state of being than it is about what we are visualising.

Visualisation is highly effective in the last twenty minutes before drifting away into the world of sleep. When we do so, we can't help waking up in a motivated mind set. Practicing visualisation daily is greatly beneficial. We are a species of habit. Repetition is the key. The more we practice visualisation, the better we will get. At the end of the day, the main thing is that you can feel what it will be like when you have your desires. That's all you are trying to do while visualising. Just feel the feelings of having it already. We become what we believe we are. It's up to you. Make up your mind.

Always remember;

IF YOU DON'T CHANGE, YOU *WILL* STAY THE SAME.

Ask yourself;

'WHERE WILL I BE IN ONE YEAR FROM NOW IF I START WORKING ON MY DREAMS DAILY FROM TODAY?'

Then, start.

NOTES

NOTES

NOTES

NOTES

NOTES

NOTES

ABOUT THE AUTHOR

My name is Abdullah Ahmad. I was born in Sligo on the 8th of November in 2001. I have 3 sisters and one brother. I moved to Dublin in 2008. I currently live near Dublin's city centre. Sometimes I still miss the family house in Sligo beside 'Strand Hill' beach although moving back wouldn't be the same.

During my primary school days, I picked up a strong interest in learning and performing magic. I wasn't anything incredible at the time, although, magic was the first form of art of which I was heavily involved and invested in. I was very committed to practicing my illusions; this was the start of my current day's self-discipline.

In my later primary school days I was introduced to the law of attraction. This impacted my life greatly. It started off my desire for personal development. Recently I found a list of my affirmations which I wrote when I was 11 years old, at the top of my list I had written; 'I am the greatest version of myself in all areas of life'.

Secondary school forced me to find myself. This, in turn, led to my self-love and self-acceptance. I learned to love myself and believe in myself. I spent hours daily on my personal development. I began to design clothes and learn business from the greats. Instead of reading school novels when I got home, I was reading books from Napoleon Hill, Jim Rohn, Donald Trump, Anthony Robins, Earl Nightingale, Dale Carnegie, Rhonda Byrne, Eckhart Tolle etc.

I currently invest hours of each day into the realisation of my desires and dreams. *When I started creating, I stopped complaining.* I realised that, DOING NOTHING DOES NOTHING. I am currently creating for the majority of my day, every day, and life is truly beautiful. I am living.

CONNECT
WITH
THE
AUTHOR

Abdullah Ahmad
Instagram: @dtmdmagician
Email: dtmdmagician@gmail.com

Joker Clothing
Instagram: @jayclothing
Email: jokerclothingofficial@gmail.com
Website: www.jokerclothing.eu

"infinite love and balance"

78705983R00076

Made in the USA
Columbia, SC
18 October 2017